This *BOOK* belongs to:

_____

_____

To my lovely friends and all our children, and the days we've spent by the sea and the days still to come when we'll listen to the waves together. N.D.

For Penny, who loves the seaside. E.S.

Nicola Davies

A FIRST BOOK
of THE SEA

Illustrated by

Emily Sutton

WALKER BOOKS
AND SUBSIDIARIES
LONDON • BOSTON • SYDNEY • AUCKLAND

Contents

Journeys

Down by the Shore

WONDERS

UNDER THE SEA

DOWN BY THE SHORE

Kick off your shoes, paddle and splash!
Surfing, swimming, making sandcastles
or just sitting and watching the waves ...
at the seaside, everything seems like fun.
But remember – the waves tell a bigger story.
Over millions of years, they have worn
rocks into the very sand
between your toes.

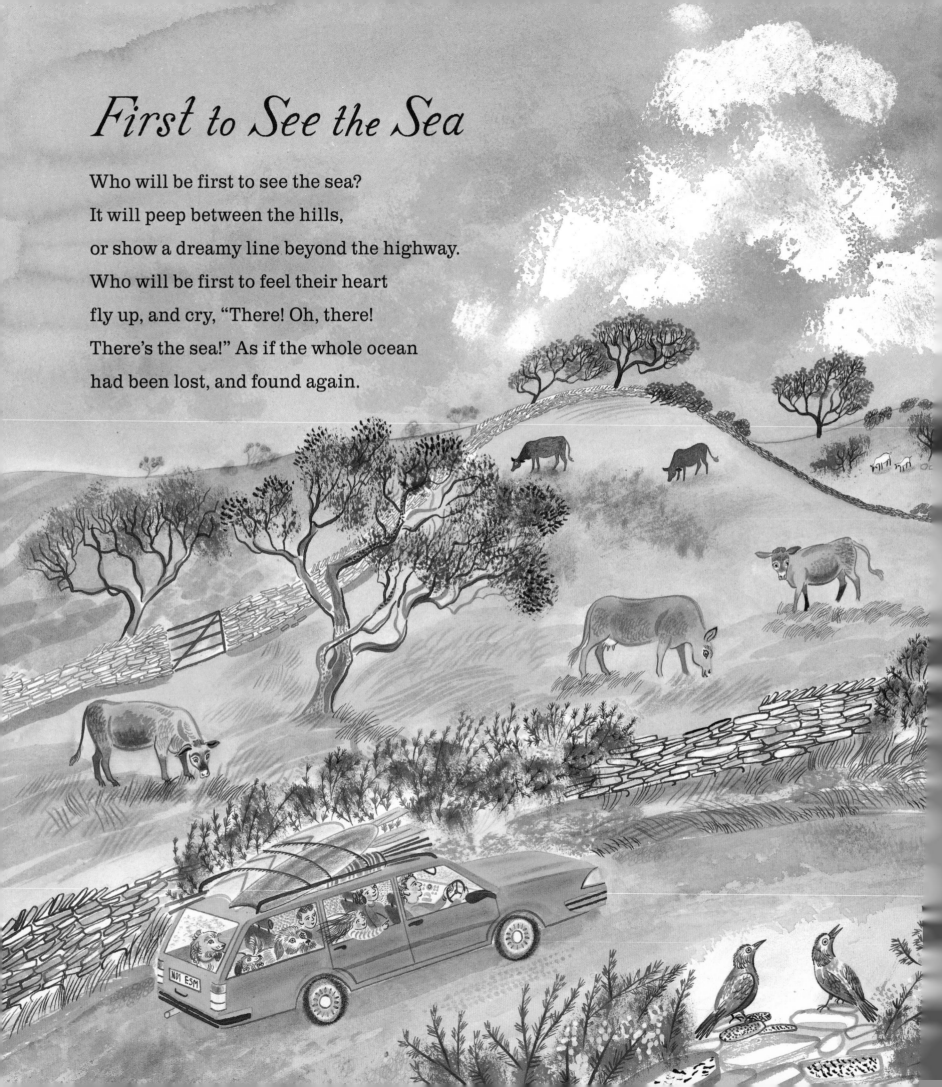

First to See the Sea

Who will be first to see the sea?
It will peep between the hills,
or show a dreamy line beyond the highway.
Who will be first to feel their heart
fly up, and cry, "There! Oh, there!
There's the sea!" As if the whole ocean
had been lost, and found again.

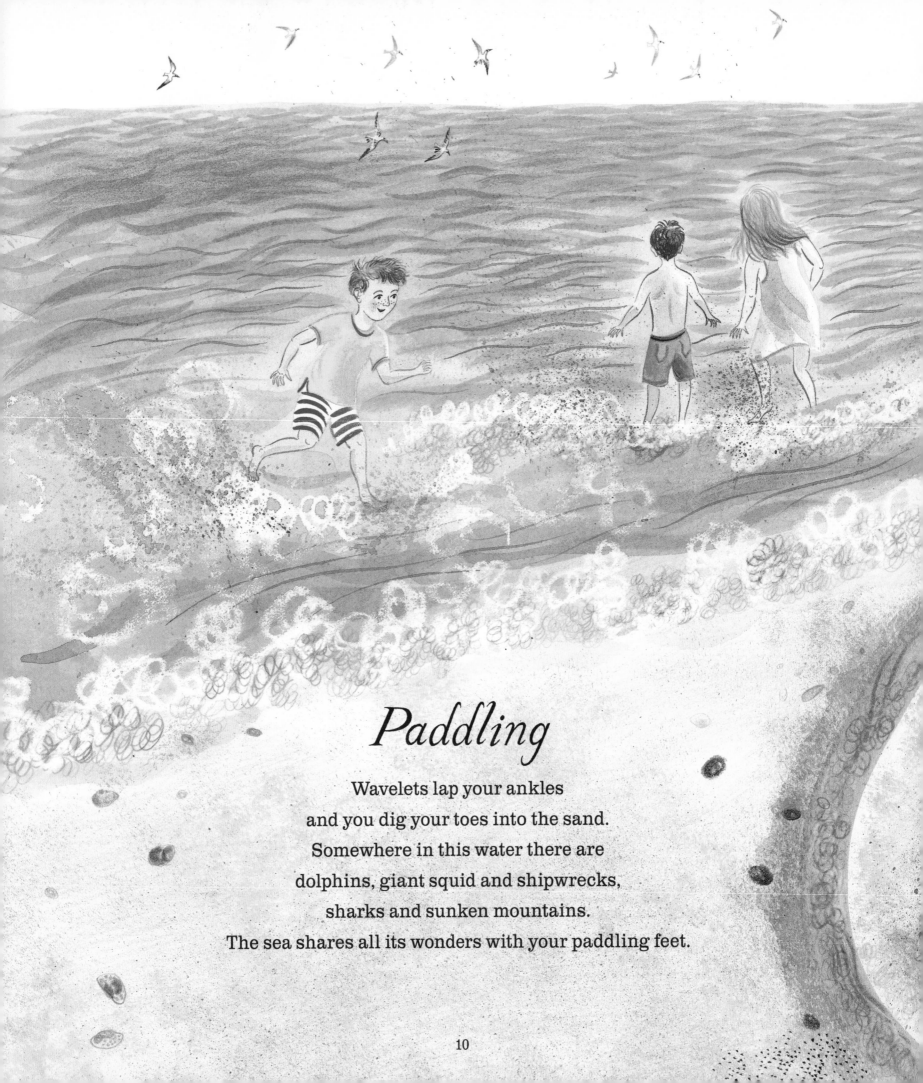

Paddling

Wavelets lap your ankles
and you dig your toes into the sand.
Somewhere in this water there are
dolphins, giant squid and shipwrecks,
sharks and sunken mountains.
The sea shares all its wonders with your paddling feet.

Sandcastle

Over the driftwood drawbridge,
along the pebble path, through the tunnels
and underneath the arches.

At last! The towers!
Their thumb-print windows stare out at the sun
and their shell front doors are closed.

Will you find the one to open
before the sea rushes from the moat?
Or tomorrow, build a different castle?

Seagulls

To stay so clean
A gull's got to preen.
Wouldn't it be better
To be brown or black or green?

No, 'cos white
Gleams very bright
So gulls in a flock
Keep their friends in sight!

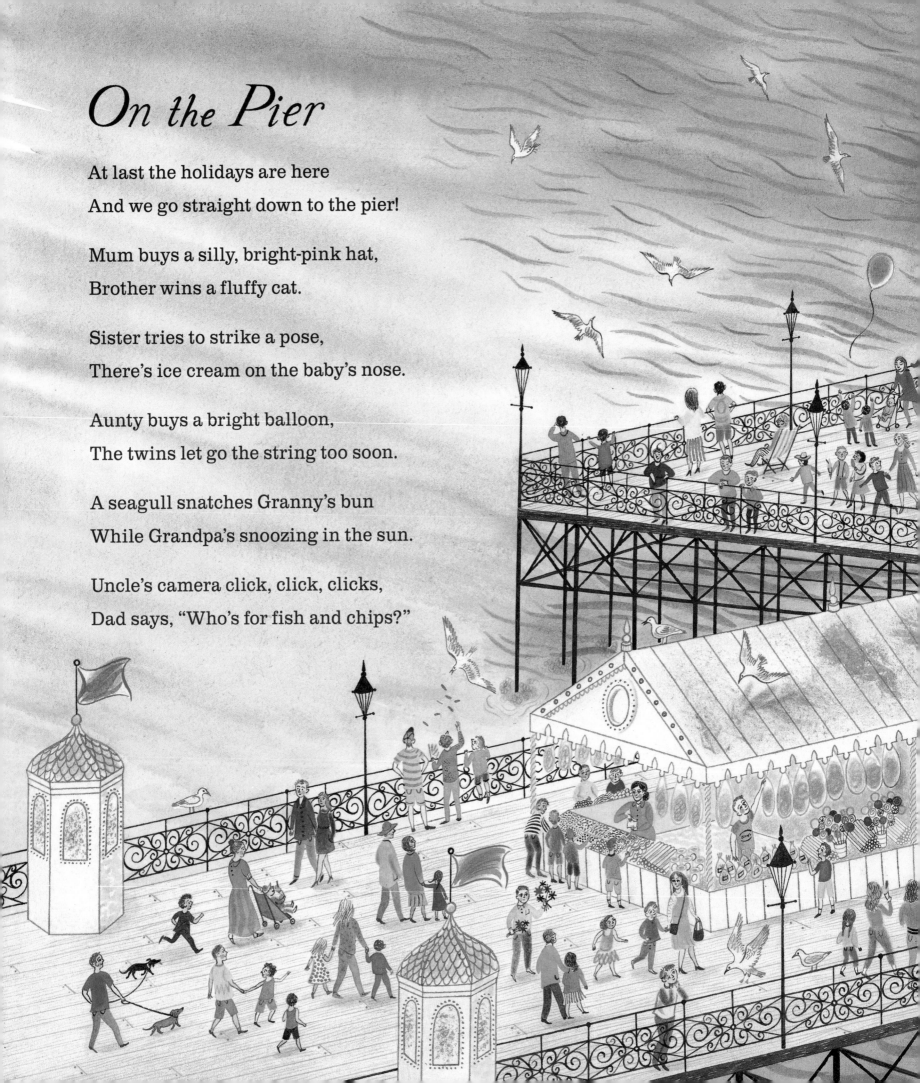

On the Pier

At last the holidays are here
And we go straight down to the pier!

Mum buys a silly, bright-pink hat,
Brother wins a fluffy cat.

Sister tries to strike a pose,
There's ice cream on the baby's nose.

Aunty buys a bright balloon,
The twins let go the string too soon.

A seagull snatches Granny's bun
While Grandpa's snoozing in the sun.

Uncle's camera click, click, clicks,
Dad says, "Who's for fish and chips?"

Waiting for the Wave

Your board bobs beyond the break zone.

On either side your feet dangle like pale fish.

In all the world there is only you.

The sky.

The sea.

This moment.

Catching a Wave

When you catch a wave, you want to shout!

When you catch a wave, you want to sing!

When you catch a wave, you want to dance!

When you catch a wave, all you want to do ...

is catch another.

Lighthouse

The light's long finger points into the darkness
to show the rocks and dangers hidden in the murk.
"Here!" says the light. "You must take care!"
Winds howl, the storm shrieks on and on.
Beneath the waves, the wrecks call,
but the light speaks, endlessly repeating:
"Here!", "Here!", "Here!"
Someone watches over you.

Puffin

I fly through the sea

easy as sunlight.

Zip! Zip!

down to where

the sand eels shiver.

Flying in thin air

is the hard part.

Tired out,

I drop onto the clifftop

wearing silver whiskers.

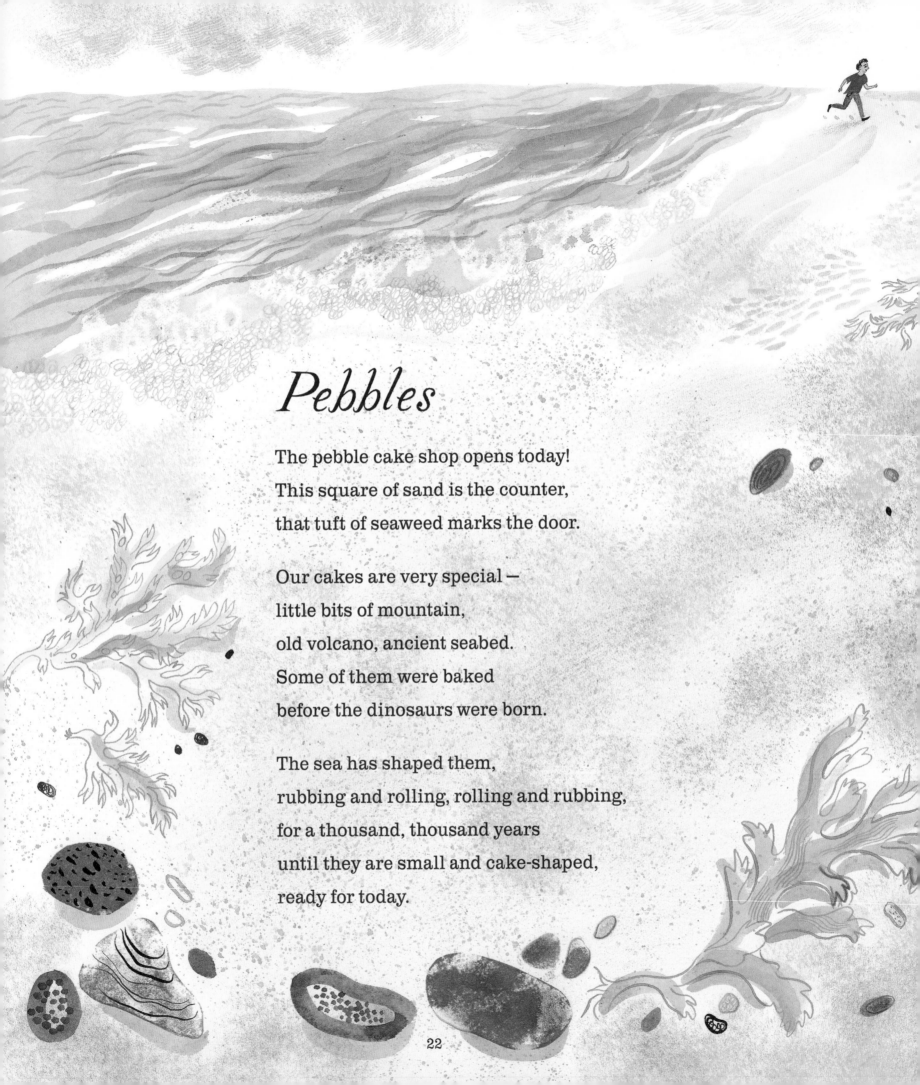

Pebbles

The pebble cake shop opens today!
This square of sand is the counter,
that tuft of seaweed marks the door.

Our cakes are very special —
little bits of mountain,
old volcano, ancient seabed.
Some of them were baked
before the dinosaurs were born.

The sea has shaped them,
rubbing and rolling, rolling and rubbing,
for a thousand, thousand years
until they are small and cake-shaped,
ready for today.

Shore Crab

Delicate!
As a dancer,
The crab sidesteps
To a dead-fish dinner.

Wary!

Periscope eyes up, watching.

Its big claws pinch tiny scraps

And pass them to its busy mouth.

Dainty!

Like a giant eating fairy cakes.

25

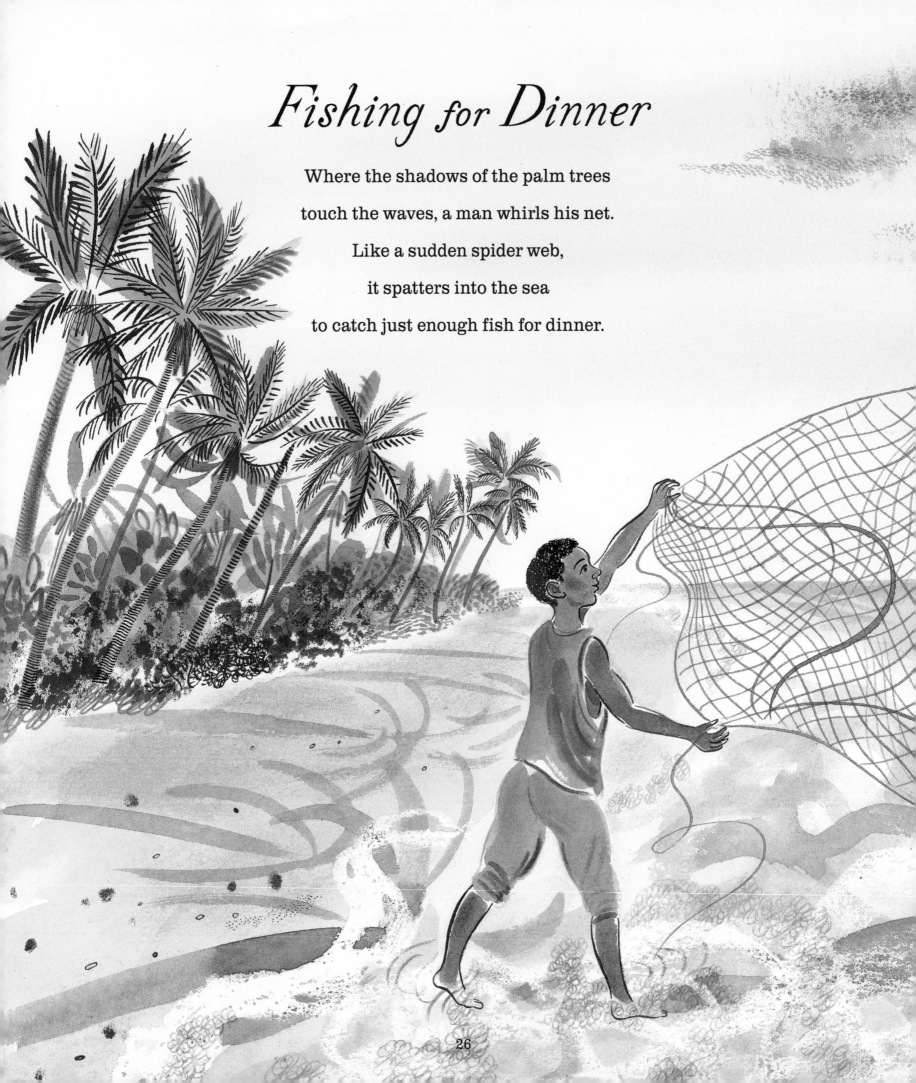

Fishing for Dinner

Where the shadows of the palm trees

touch the waves, a man whirls his net.

Like a sudden spider web,

it spatters into the sea

to catch just enough fish for dinner.

26

I Love Harbours

I love the smell of harbours,
Seaweed, engine oil and fish.
I love the way that rigging rattles in the wind
And hulls squeak against their fenders.
I love the massive chugging of the big container ships
As they shoulder out between the buoys.
I love the promise of adventures
Out there on the sea!

Finding Shells

There's no special trick to finding seashells.

All you have to do is look.

It's hard at first, but soon your eyes

will start to notice tiny details

and you'll pick up little bits of beauty.

Let your heart sing for a moment,

then put them back:

someone else might need them.

All Day

We watched the waves all day.
We watched the splash and tangle
and the way the foam clung on
among the rocks.

We listened to the crash,
the hollow booming of their breaking,
the sizzling hiss of backwash.

We watched the waves all day
and didn't say a word,
then walked home, hand in hand.

JOURNEYS

The sea is full of journeys, from the
long migrations of whales to the tiny
trips of limpets across a rock.
Humans too have been criss-crossing
the oceans for thousands of years,
in search of new homes, to explore
the planet or simply to experience
the thrill of a voyage.

Sea Shanty

To roam the seas you catch the wind.

Pull now! Away oh!

To catch the wind you raise a sail.

Pull now! Away oh!

To raise a sail you haul a rope.

Pull now! Away oh!

To haul a rope you sing a song.

Pull now! Away oh!

To sing a song you catch the wind.

Pull now! Away oh!

To catch the wind you roam the seas.

Pull now! Away oh!

Limpets

Limpets live on tide time.
When the tide is in, they get up and walk —
just a little way — less than your arm's length.
When the tide goes out, they walk right back
and clamp their shells tight against the rock,
until the tide turns and the sea comes back:
time for another little walk!

Blue Whale's Map

Blue whales don't know much
about the land, but they can go
from Chile to China,
from Alaska to Australia,
and still be in their kingdom.
So who knows more about
the world and what it's made of —
you or a blue whale?

The Voyages of Captain Zheng He

From China to Africa

Four hundred years ago

Sailed bold Captain Zheng

Dreaming dragon spit and incense

And amber shining like the sun

In a ship with nine tall masts

And sails as big as whales

Sailed bold Captain Zheng

Trading dragon spit and incense

And amber shining like the sun

Home again to China

With a live giraffe aboard

Sailed bold Captain Zheng

Singing dragon spit and incense

And amber shining like the sun

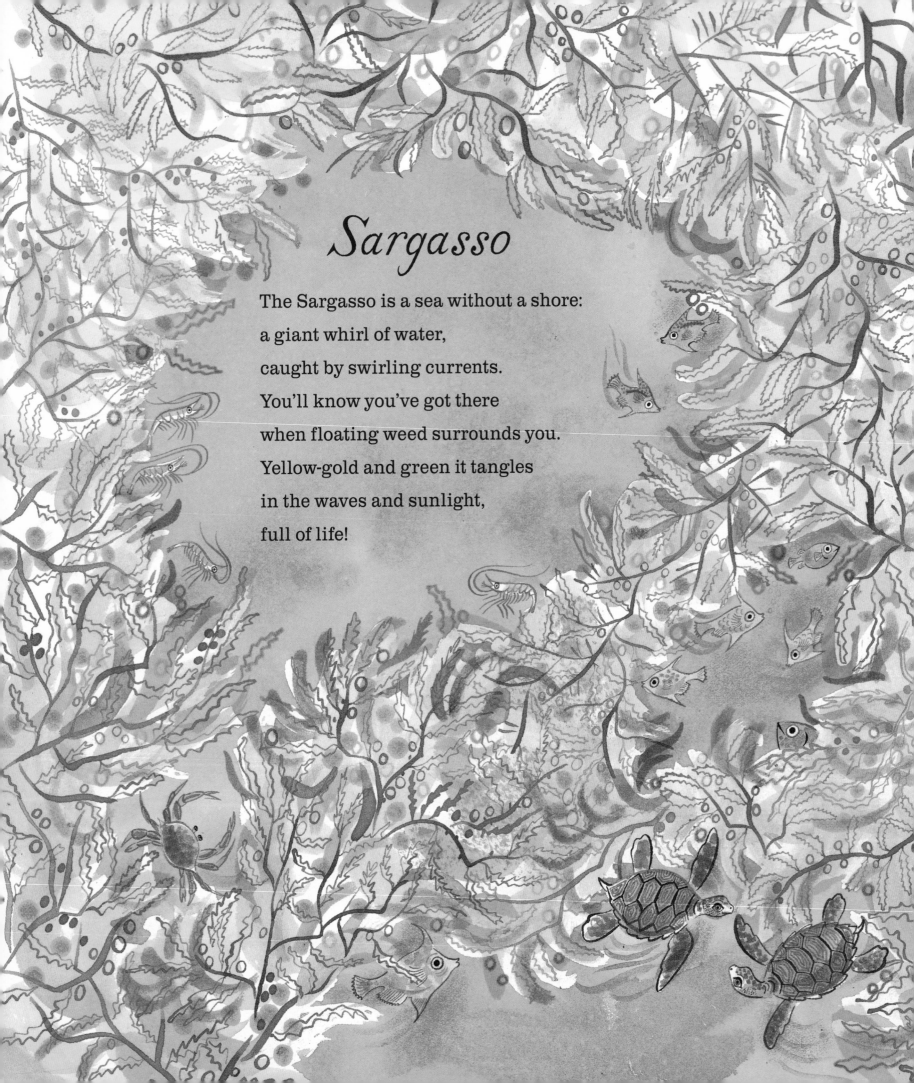

Sargasso

The Sargasso is a sea without a shore:

a giant whirl of water,

caught by swirling currents.

You'll know you've got there

when floating weed surrounds you.

Yellow-gold and green it tangles

in the waves and sunlight,

full of life!

Elver

See-through, fragile as a fallen leaf,
smaller than your finger.
Yet it will swim across an ocean
to find a muddy river mouth,
a place to become itself: an eel.

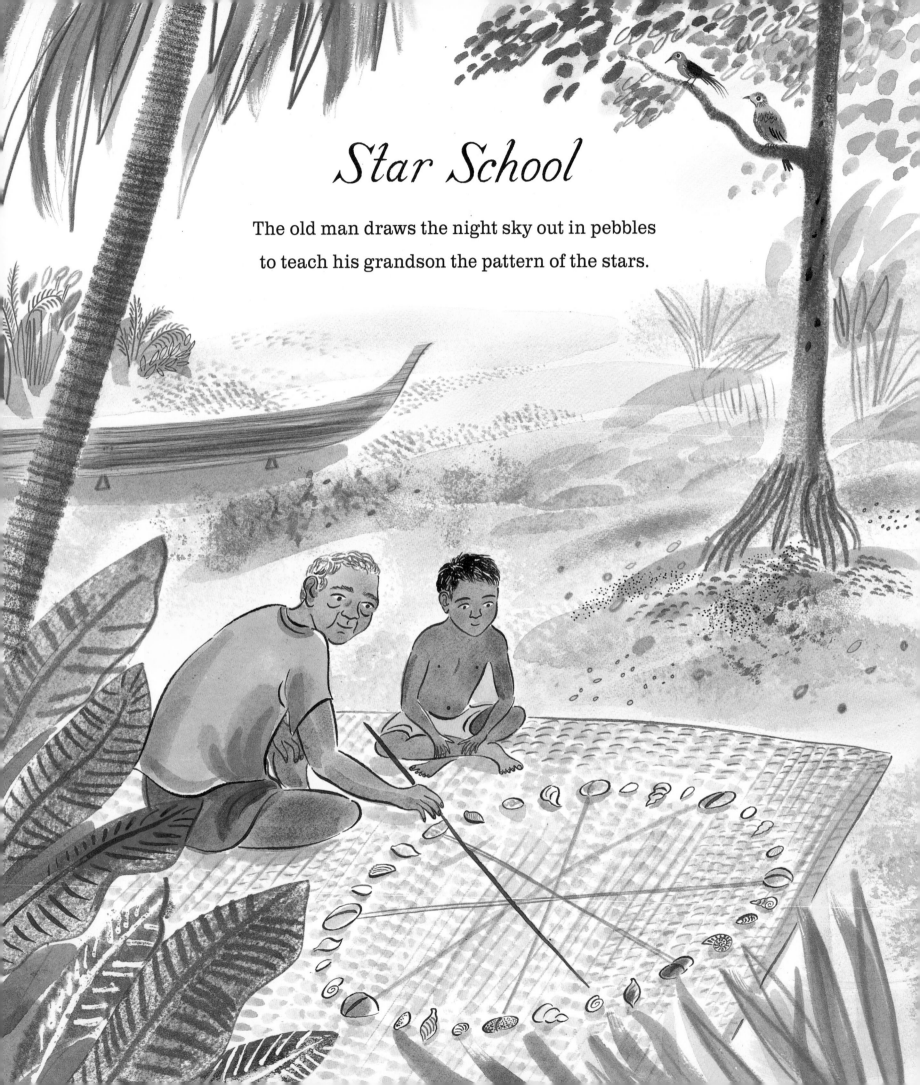

Star School

The old man draws the night sky out in pebbles
to teach his grandson the pattern of the stars.

They will steer his path across the ocean

like stepping stones laid out in the sky.

They'll steer him safe to tiny islands,

green stars lost in seas of blue.

Sea Turtle

It was a flat calm day and we floated

on water at least three thousand metres deep,

and two day's sail to any land.

A turtle, smaller than a soup dish,

passed us by. It swam on and on,

and disappeared from sight.

From horizon to horizon

there was nothing but the sea

and that small turtle,

steering its straight, sure course.

Lord Beaufort's Scale

From one to twelve runs Beaufort's Scale
To tell ships when it's safe to sail.

Up to four, the sea is flat
And winds would not disturb a hat.

By five or six white crests of foam
Tell small boats that it's time for home.

By eight or nine, upon the scale,
Big ships will struggle in the gale.

At ten, waves are house-high and steep;
The storm spray streaks across the deep.

With waves that break like falling towers
Twelve shows the hurricane's vast powers.

Somewhere far away from home
A sailor listens, all alone,
Ear to a crackly radio,
For numbers that all sailors know.
The one to twelve of Beaufort's Scale
That tells ships when it's safe to sail!

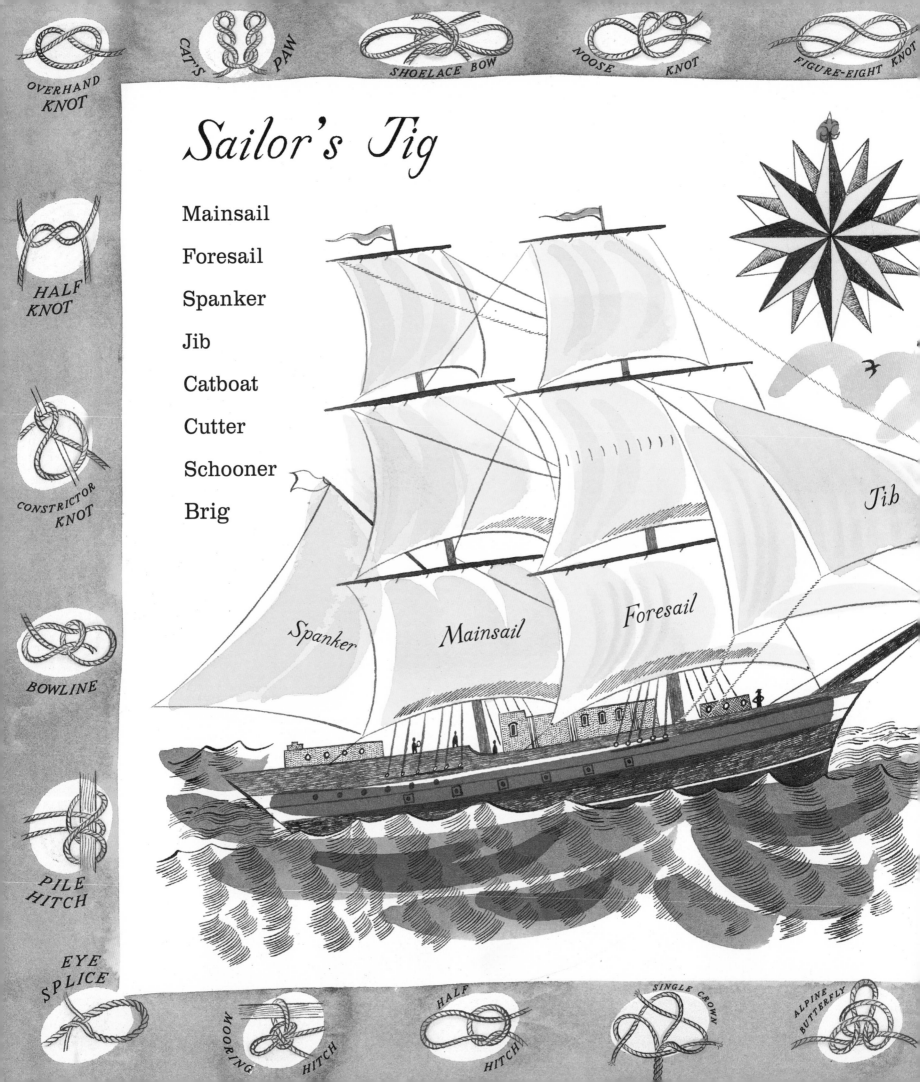

Sailor's Jig

Mainsail

Foresail

Spanker

Jib

Catboat

Cutter

Schooner

Brig

OVERHAND KNOT

CAT'S PAW

SHOELACE BOW

NOOSE KNOT

FIGURE-EIGHT KNOT

HALF KNOT

CONSTRICTOR KNOT

BOWLINE

PILE HITCH

EYE SPLICE

MOORING HITCH

HALF HITCH

SINGLE CROWN

ALPINE BUTTERFLY KNOT

Spanker   Mainsail   Foresail   Jib

SLIP KNOT   SHEET BEND   OPEN CHAIN   DOUBLE OVERHAND   ANCHOR HITCH

BALE SLING HITCH

ZEPPELIN BEND

STEVEDORE KNOT

CARRICK BEND

FISHERMAN'S KNOT

CATBOAT

CUTTER

SCHOONER

BRIG

GRANNY KNOT   COW HITCH   FISHERMAN'S EYE   PRUSIK KNOT

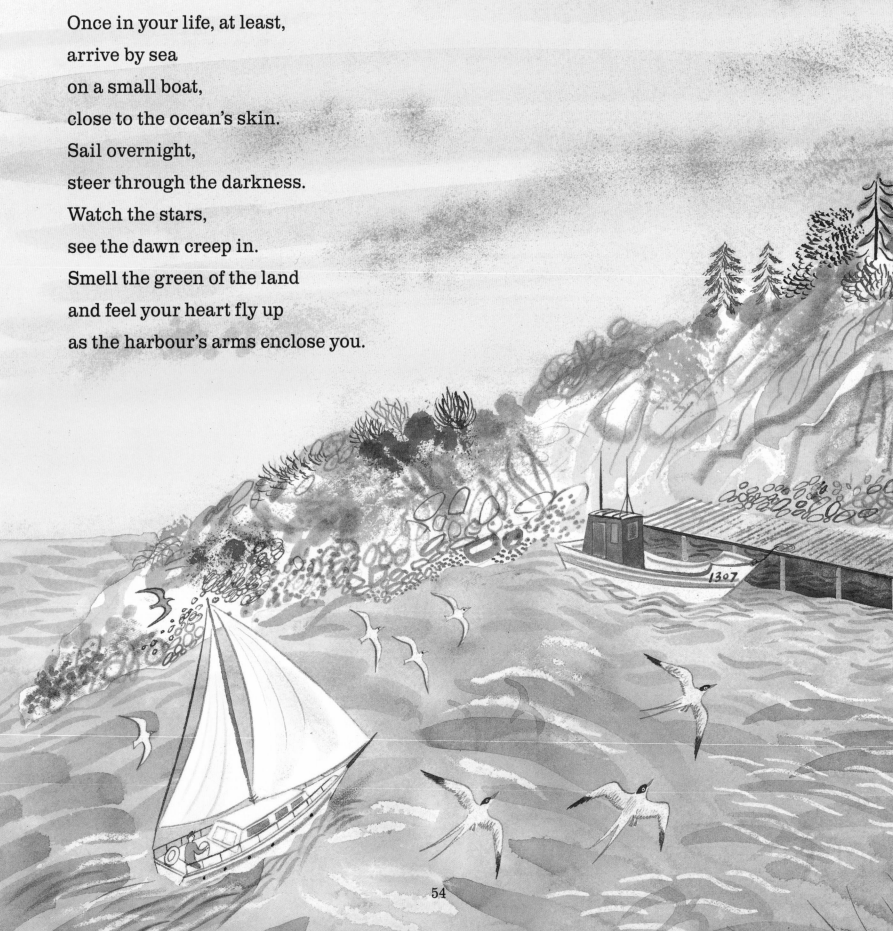

End of the Journey

Once in your life, at least,

arrive by sea

on a small boat,

close to the ocean's skin.

Sail overnight,

steer through the darkness.

Watch the stars,

see the dawn creep in.

Smell the green of the land

and feel your heart fly up

as the harbour's arms enclose you.

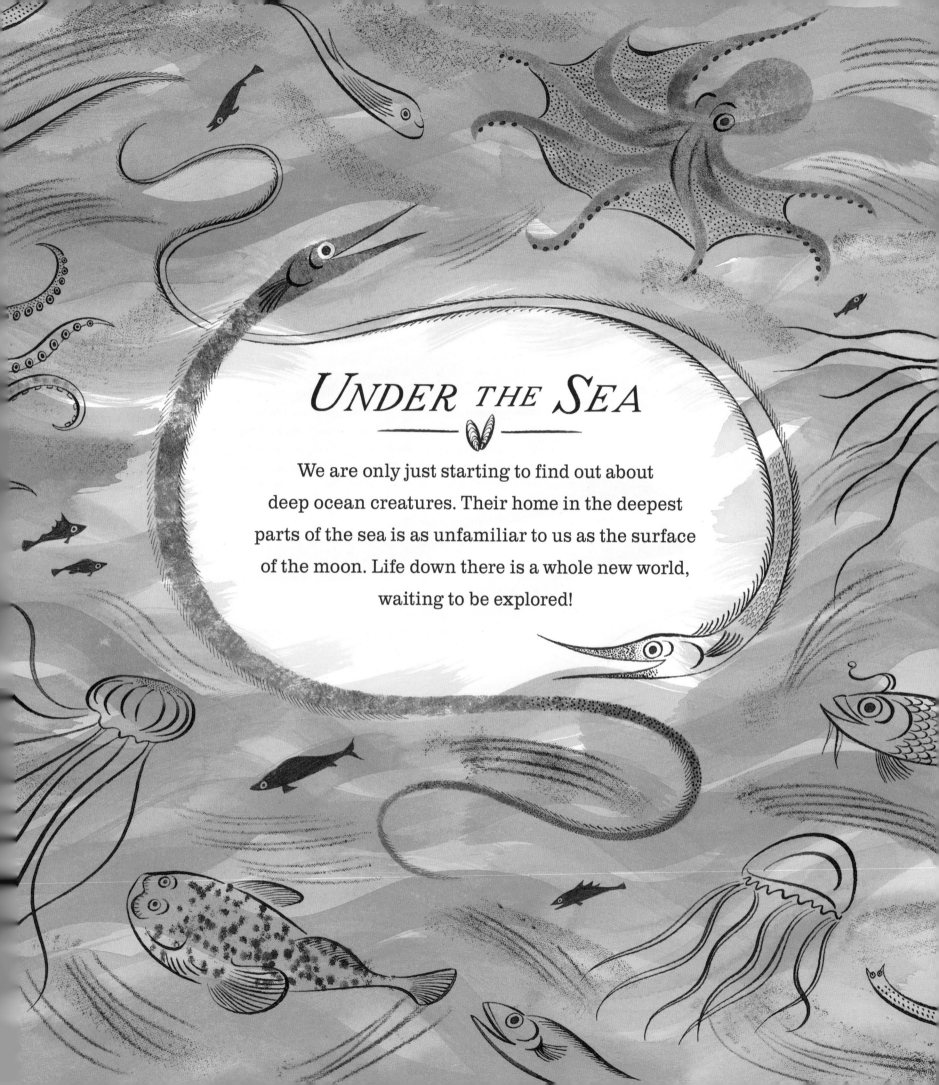

UNDER THE SEA

We are only just starting to find out about
deep ocean creatures. Their home in the deepest
parts of the sea is as unfamiliar to us as the surface
of the moon. Life down there is a whole new world,
waiting to be explored!

Deep

Down! Deep and deeper.
Down to where it's always dark and cold.
So deep the weight of water up above you
could squish you like a bug.

Things loom into the circle of your lights —
half-seen giants, things that glow,
un-named creatures with strange shapes.
You feel you are an alien in their world.

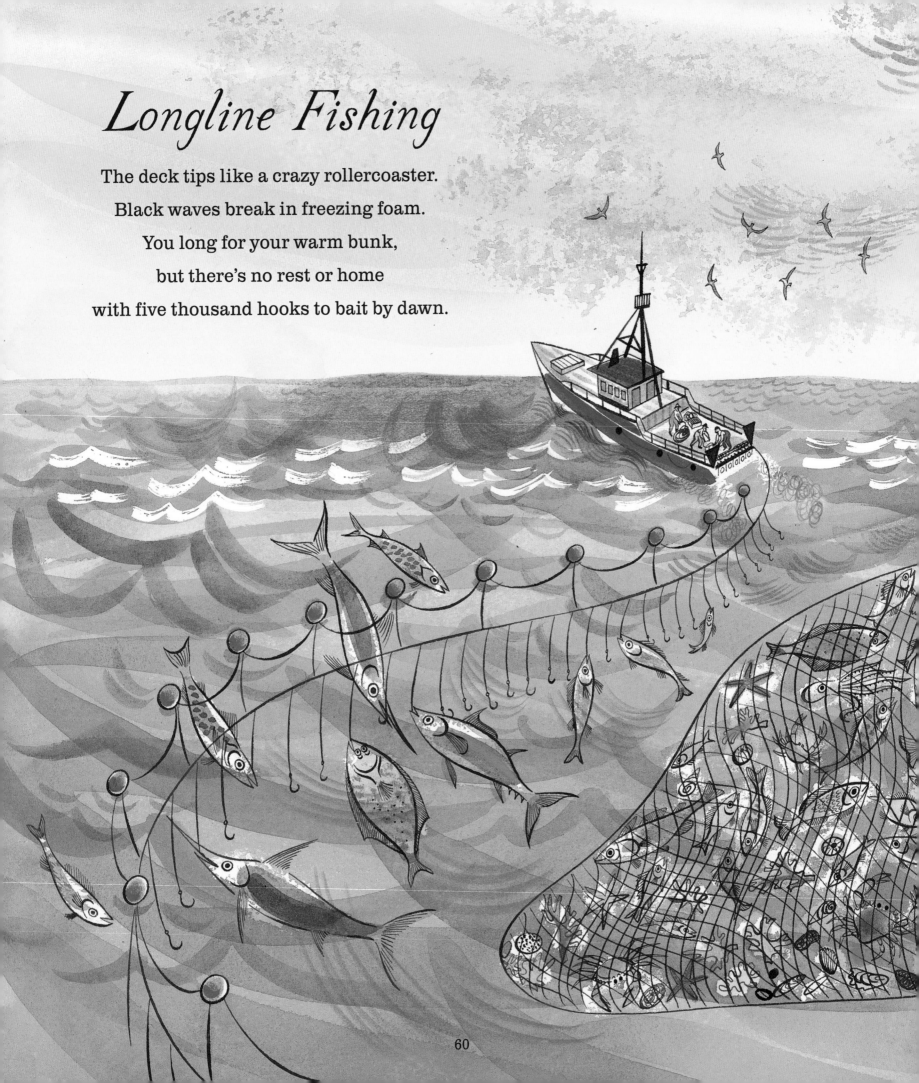

Longline Fishing

The deck tips like a crazy rollercoaster.

Black waves break in freezing foam.

You long for your warm bunk,

but there's no rest or home

with five thousand hooks to bait by dawn.

Bottom Trawling

The monster net takes everything:

big fish, small fish,

crabs and shells and corals.

Nothing's left but a dead and empty wasteland

where plastic bottles sink into the mud.

Giant Squid

"The giant squid's a fearsome beast
Five hundred metres long at least.
It swallows ships in just one bite
You'd look at it and die of fright!"

Well, that's the myth, now here's the truth,
Caught on camera for proof,
Giant squid are rather fine,
With a lovely, silvery shine,
And massive eyes like dinner dishes
And tentacles for catching fishes.
It's true they are quite big, but note,
Not big enough to eat a boat.

Deadliest of All?

The blue-ringed octopus perhaps?
Whose little bite you'd hardly feel ...
until it killed you.

A tiger shark?
With rows of teeth
to slice you into bits.

A sea wasp jellyfish?
The stings of just a single tentacle
could end your life.

No! Deadliest of all
is the plastic we throw away
that strangles, suffocates and poisons.

Flashlight Fish

A festival of flashlight fish!

On-off, off-on.

It's a Morse code fiesta

of living lanterns.

Arctic Ocean

Ice is the sky of the Arctic Ocean,
carved by currents into
columns, curves and pyramids.
Polar bears peer down,
seals swoop, krill cluster,
and the songs of bowhead whales
twine and echo in the blue twilight.

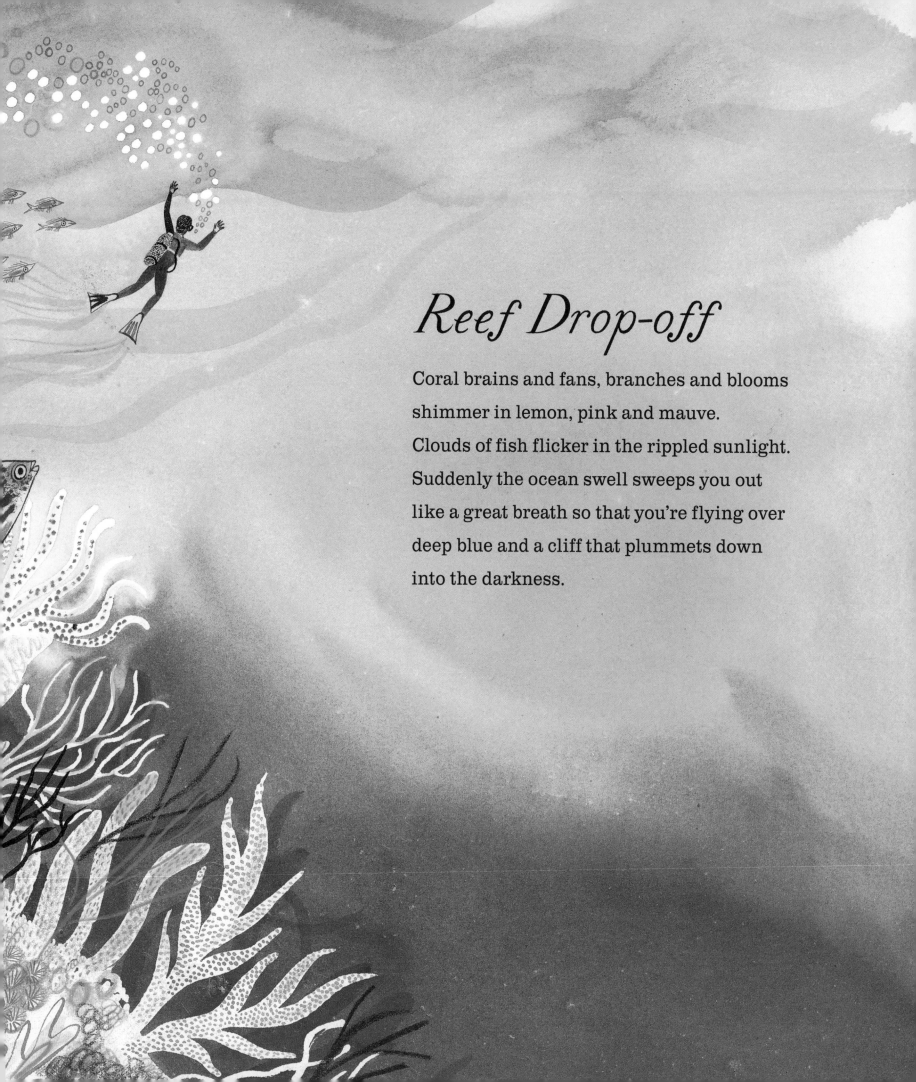

Reef Drop-off

Coral brains and fans, branches and blooms
shimmer in lemon, pink and mauve.
Clouds of fish flicker in the rippled sunlight.
Suddenly the ocean swell sweeps you out
like a great breath so that you're flying over
deep blue and a cliff that plummets down
into the darkness.

Anglerfish

Deep down,

where it's always midnight,

a nightmare lurks,

luring victims with a little light,

until they're close enough

for the needle teeth

and gaping mouth to reach.

Are you afraid?
You don't need to be —
this bad dream could
barely bite your big toe!

Sharks

We shiver when the slick shark

slides through the shadows,

searching, searching.

But without that sleek shape

the salt seas would be less —

like the land without lions.

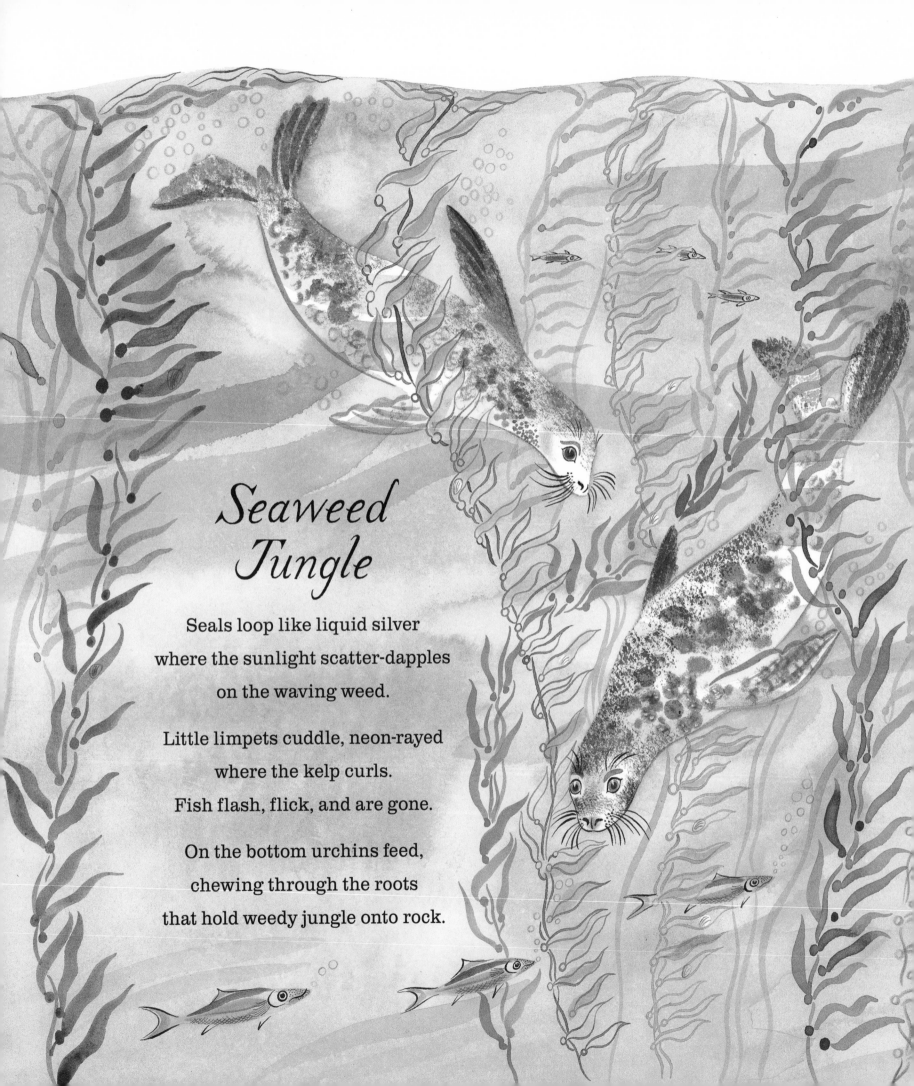

Seaweed Jungle

Seals loop like liquid silver
where the sunlight scatter-dapples
on the waving weed.

Little limpets cuddle, neon-rayed
where the kelp curls.
Fish flash, flick, and are gone.

On the bottom urchins feed,
chewing through the roots
that hold weedy jungle onto rock.

Mother Sea Otter

Round she rolls her bobbing baby,
Wrapping him in seaweed strands
To keep him anchored while she dives
For abalones, urchins, clams.

Shipwreck

The wooden ship, her sailors' bones — long gone.

But the clay pots she carried lie on the seabed

like a clutch of broken eggs.

They still hold the ghostly traces of her cargo —

oil and olives, perfume, fish —

that tell us now the story of her journeys

and of her crew, lost here

three thousand years ago.

WONDERS

You might never swim with a manta ray
or watch penguins leaping between the Antarctic
ice floes. But the sea-worn pebble in your pocket
reminds you that these magical things
are out there, somewhere on our beautiful
blue planet ... perhaps waiting just
over the horizon.

Rockpool

Sand is for playing.

Rockpools are for explorers.

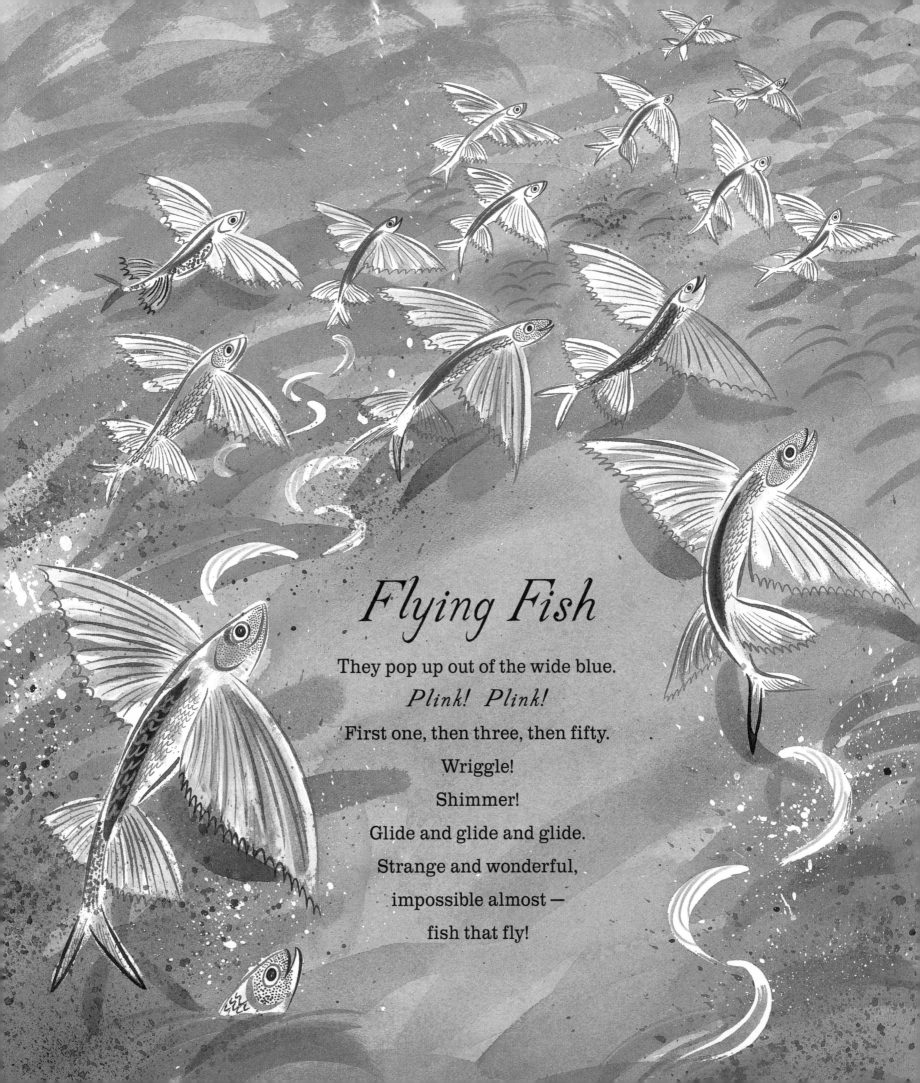

Flying Fish

They pop up out of the wide blue.

Plink! Plink!

First one, then three, then fifty.

Wriggle!

Shimmer!

Glide and glide and glide.

Strange and wonderful,

impossible almost —

fish that fly!

Night Light

Sometimes in the sea, at night,
creatures small enough
to swim through a needle's eye
flash their little light
when something scares them.

Then, your boat,

sailing suddenly through the water,

leaves a neon trail, glowing,

all the way to morning.

Antarctic

On the seabed, starfish shine like flowers.
Penguins shoot up in trails of bubbles,
and flop out, flipper-flapping on the floes.
Leopard seals lurk between ice pancakes
and wild waves worry at the glacier's edge,
biting off icebergs that splash in the bay.

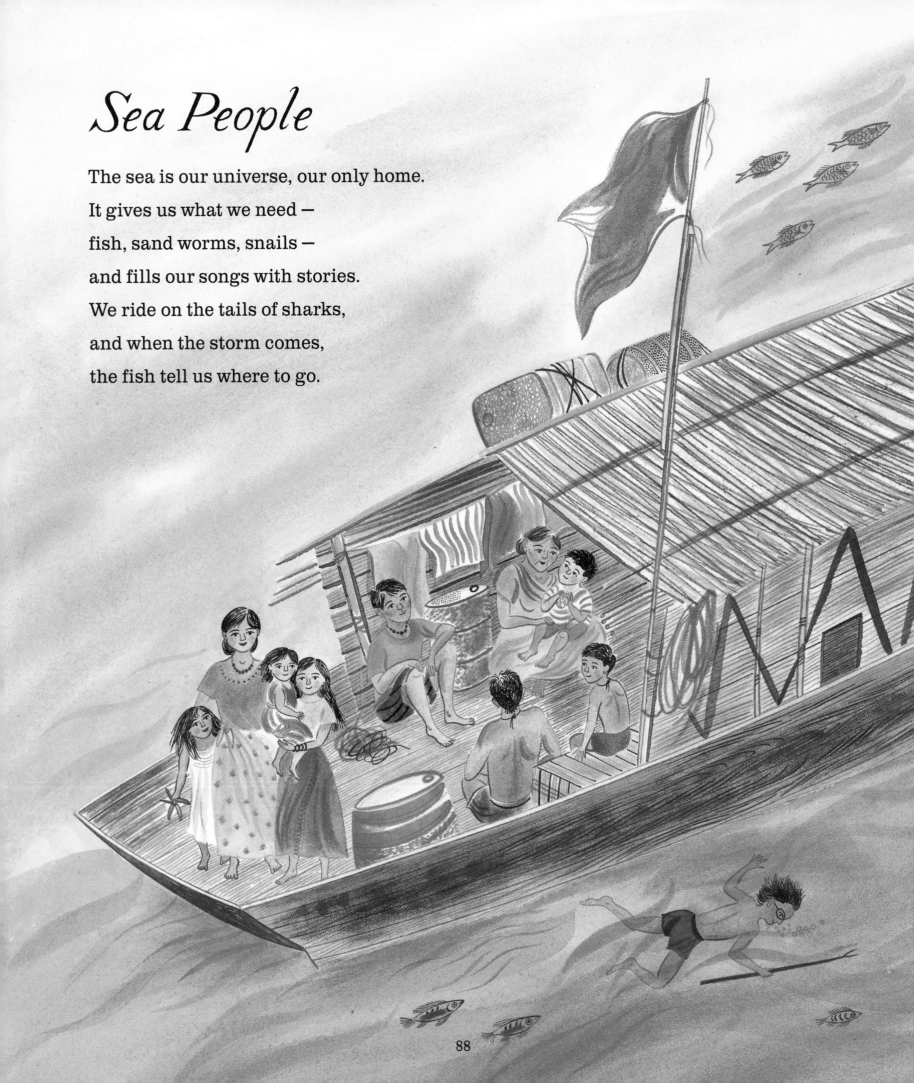

Sea People

The sea is our universe, our only home.

It gives us what we need —

fish, sand worms, snails —

and fills our songs with stories.

We ride on the tails of sharks,

and when the storm comes,

the fish tell us where to go.

Albatross

House-high waves

and icebergs big enough

to be small countries.

Winds that scream and whip the sea

into a foam that fills the air.

Weather like a war zone!

The albatross holds it all

in its dark, quiet eye,

and glides calmly down the gale.

Shoal

Swirl, swish.   Twirl, twist.   Flash, flick.   Gleam, glint.

All turn, all dive, all eyes open wide.

Ten thousand bodies move in time,

A moving, swimming, living rhyme.

Favourite Dolphin

Choose just one?
It's impossible to pick!

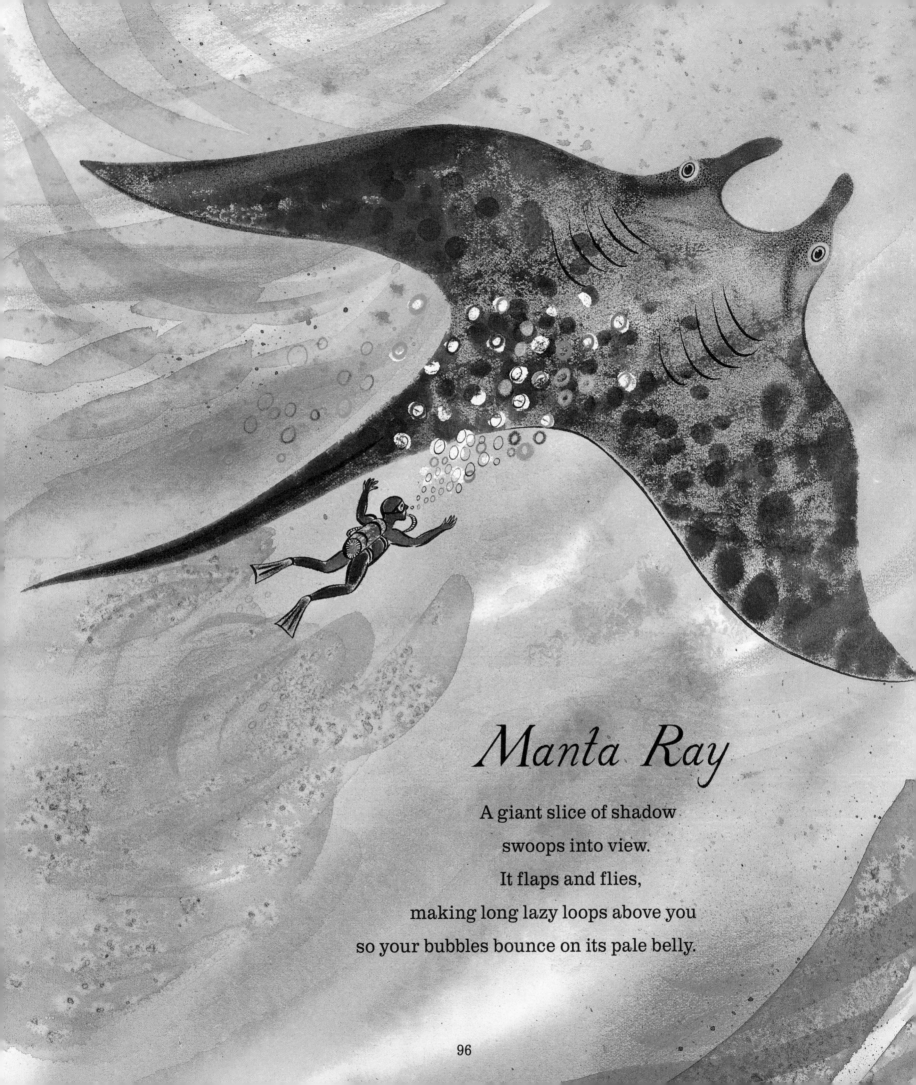

Manta Ray

A giant slice of shadow

swoops into view.

It flaps and flies,

making long lazy loops above you

so your bubbles bounce on its pale belly.

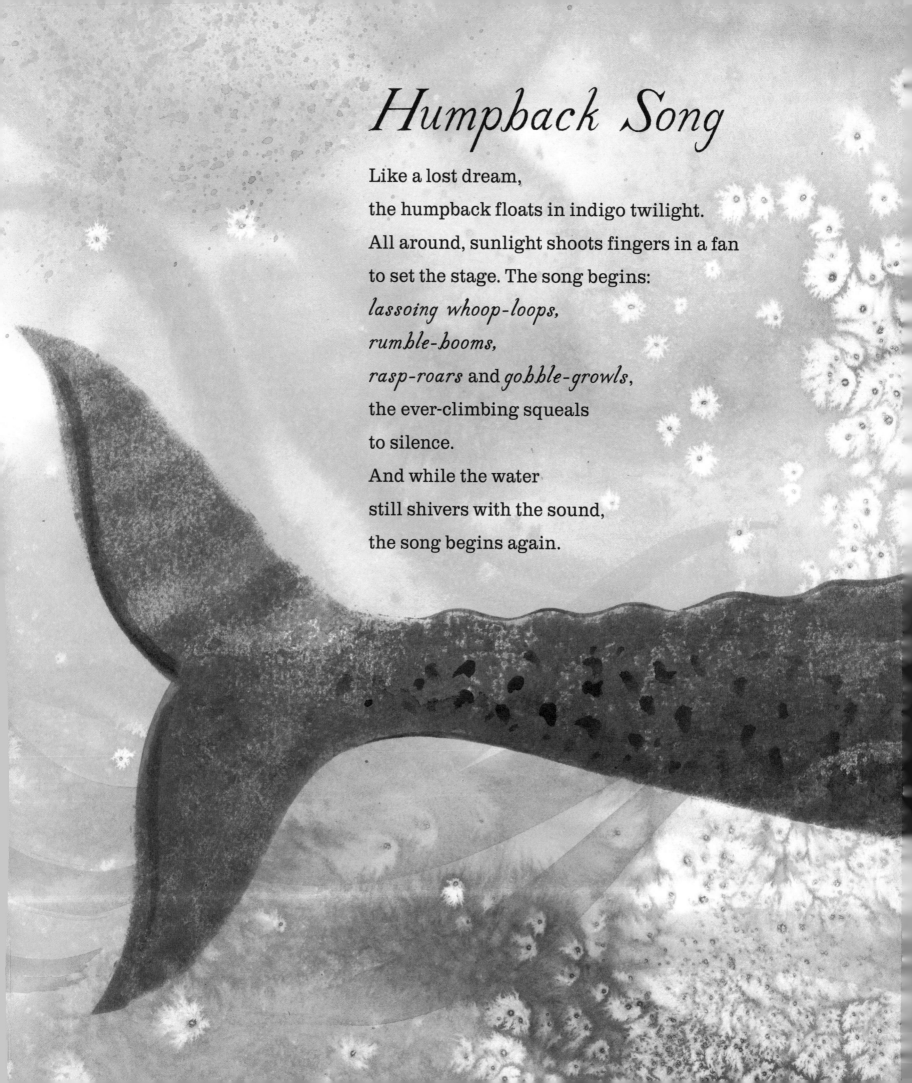

Humpback Song

Like a lost dream,

the humpback floats in indigo twilight.

All around, sunlight shoots fingers in a fan

to set the stage. The song begins:

lassoing whoop-loops,

rumble-booms,

rasp-roars and *gobble-growls,*

the ever-climbing squeals

to silence.

And while the water

still shivers with the sound,

the song begins again.

Pearl Diver

Inside the diver's eye, the sea.

Inside the sea, the tangled weed.

Inside the weed, the oyster shell.

Inside the oyster shell, the pearl.

Inside the pearl, the diver's eye.

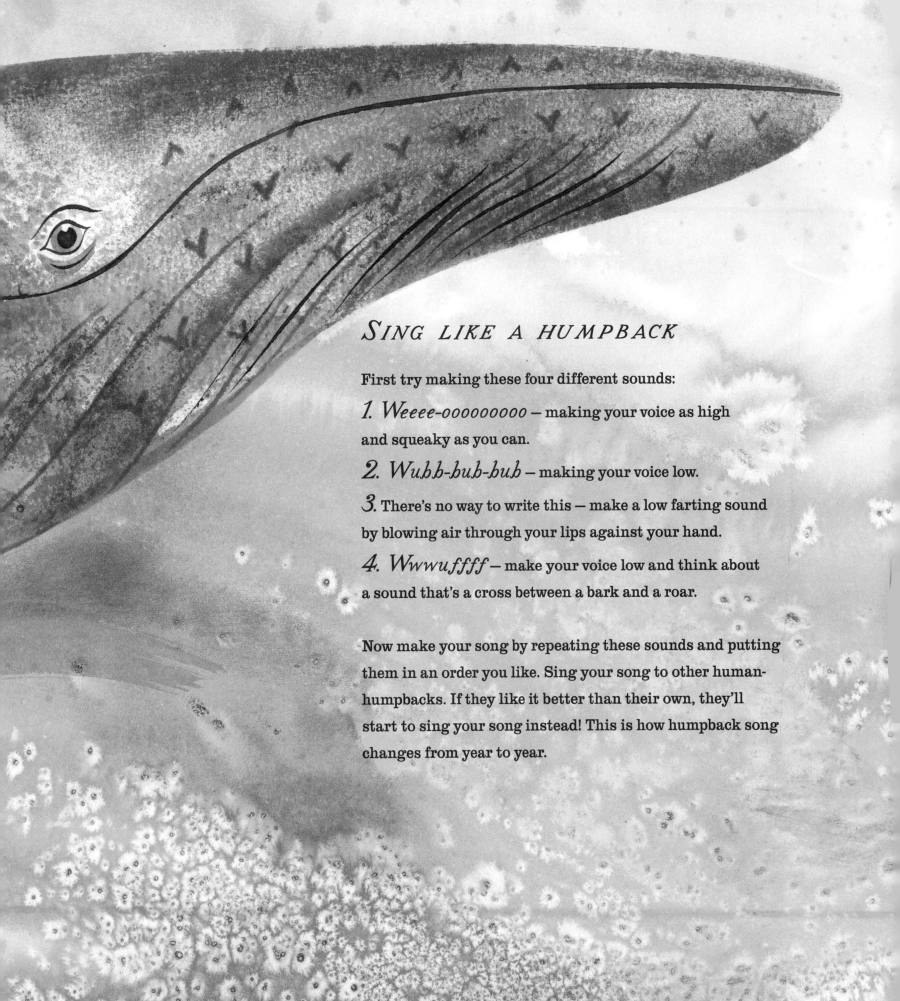

SING LIKE A HUMPBACK

First try making these four different sounds:

1. Weeee-ooooooooo — making your voice as high and squeaky as you can.

2. Wubb-bub-bub — making your voice low.

3. There's no way to write this — make a low farting sound by blowing air through your lips against your hand.

4. Wwwuffff — make your voice low and think about a sound that's a cross between a bark and a roar.

Now make your song by repeating these sounds and putting them in an order you like. Sing your song to other human-humpbacks. If they like it better than their own, they'll start to sing your song instead! This is how humpback song changes from year to year.

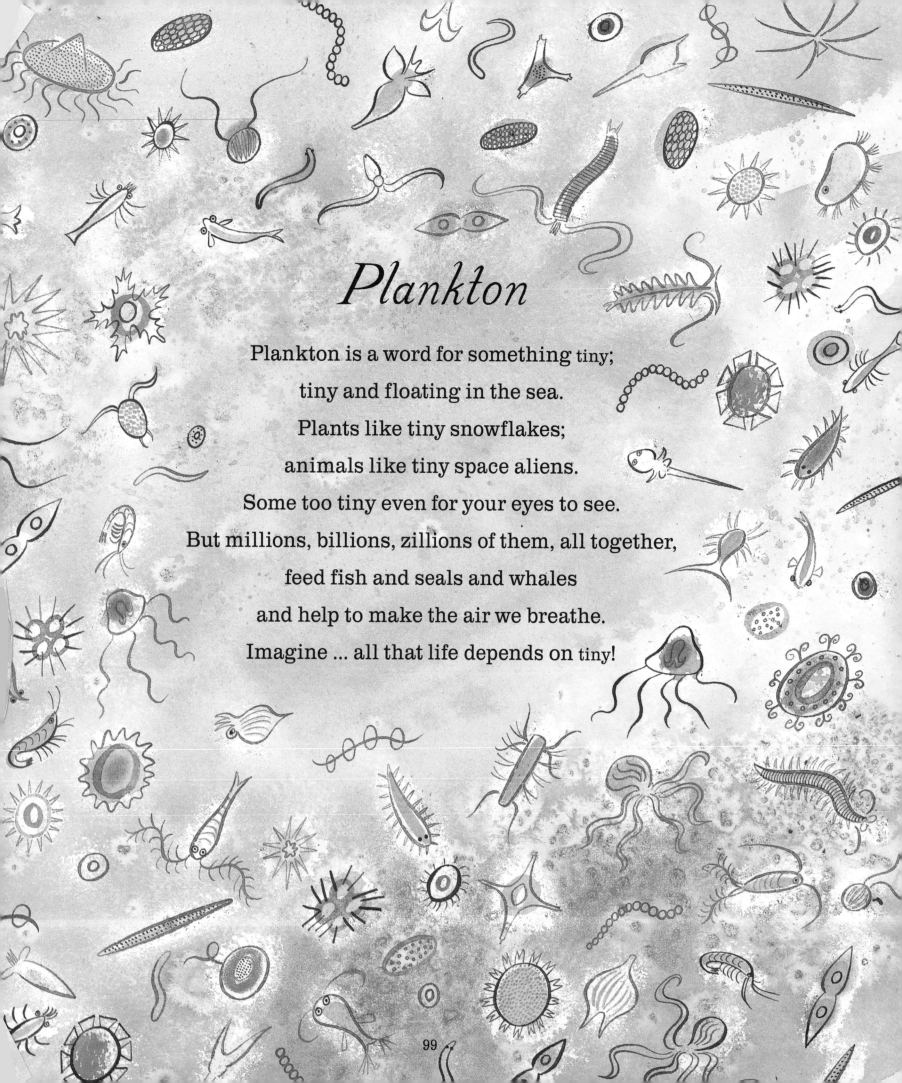

Plankton

Plankton is a word for something tiny;

tiny and floating in the sea.

Plants like tiny snowflakes;

animals like tiny space aliens.

Some too tiny even for your eyes to see.

But millions, billions, zillions of them, all together,

feed fish and seals and whales

and help to make the air we breathe.

Imagine ... all that life depends on tiny!

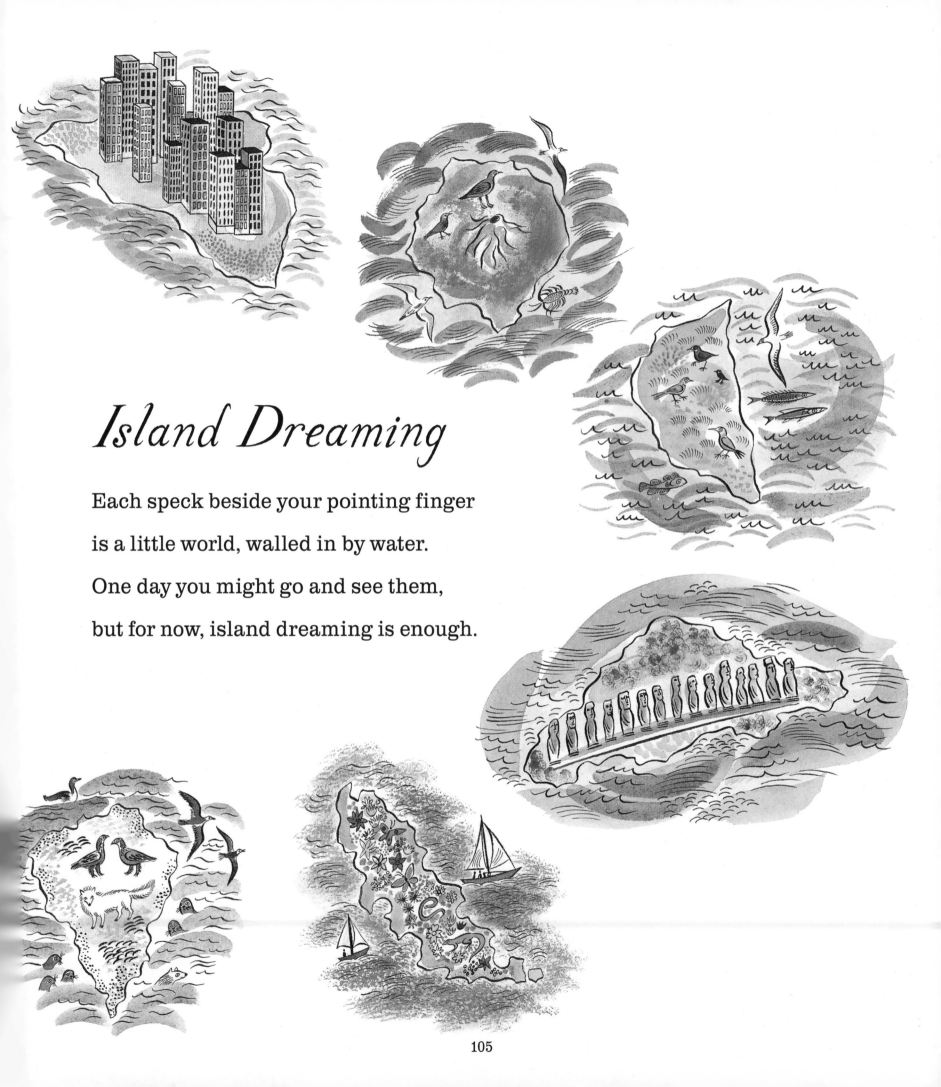

Island Dreaming

Each speck beside your pointing finger

is a little world, walled in by water.

One day you might go and see them,

but for now, island dreaming is enough.

Happiness

Sand in my shoes.

Salt in my hair.

A pebble in my pocket.

The horizon in my eyes.

First published 2018 by Walker Books Ltd
87 Vauxhall Walk, London SE11 5HJ

2 4 6 8 10 9 7 5 3 1

Text © 2018 Nicola Davies Illustrations © 2018 Emily Sutton

The right of Nicola Davies and Emily Sutton to be identified as author
and illustrator respectively of this work has been asserted by them
in accordance with the Copyright, Designs and Patents Act 1988

This book has been typeset in Clarendon

Printed and bound in China

British Library Cataloguing in Publication Data:
a catalogue record for this book is available from the British Library

ISBN 978-1-4063-6895-6

www.walker.co.uk